FACE YOUR FEELINGS!

A Book to Help Children Learn About Feelings

Concept developed by Lawrence E. Shapiro, Ph.D.

Childswork™ Childsplay

CALL 1·800·962·1141

A Brand of The Guidance Group
www.guidance-group.com

FACE YOUR FEELINGS!
Concept developed by Lawrence. E. Shapiro

Childswork/Childsplay publishes products for mental health professionals, teachers, and parents who wish to help children with their developmental, social, and emotional growth. For questions, comments, or to request a free catalog describing hundreds of games, toys, books, and other counseling tools, call 1-800-962-1141

Copyright ©1993 by Childswork/Childsplay
A Brand of The Guidance Group
www.guidance-group.com
1-800-962-1141

ISBN10: 1-882732-07-3
ISBN 13: 978-1-882732-07-4

DEDICATION

This book is dedicated to my mother, Frances Shapiro, who, through her generosity of spirit and heart, has provided the inspiration for this project and everything else worthwhile that I have done

— Lawrence E. Shapiro, Ph.D.

ACKNOWLEDGEMENTS

Our thanks to our terrifically expressive models:

Sultana Alam	Jessica Lamb-Shapiro	Joseph Shore
Jason Allen	Jonathan Lawrence	Robin Shore
Samiul Amin	Laura Lawrence	Patricia Smith
Darryl Anderson	Gary Lynch	David Snyder
Kevin Black	Cierra Magobet	Kate Stackhouse
Leah Bustard	Deborah Marine	Kevin Stackhouse
Alex Claypool	Walter Marine	Renee Stein
John Davis	Darren Monroe	Rubin Stein
Kaya Davis	Eric Murray	Jennifer Steptoe
Stephanie Elson	Adrienne Pancoe	Abbe Stern
Rita Ann Gold	Rezina Quddus	Elise Stern
Lisa Horton	Brad Ruben Winter	Mitchell Stern
Emily Hughes	Christopher Ryan	Alene Tchourumoff
Mary Hughes	Jordan Shapiro	TJ Trinidad
Greg Hymel	Chi Hoon Shin	Beth Ann Wakely
John Joyner	Andrew Shore	Rena Womack
Ian Kelly	Bette Shore	Pei Li Xu
Dorothy Kennedy		

Thanks also to the people who made this book happen:

Concept: Lawrence E. Shapiro, Ph.D.   Book Design and Layout: Christopher Laughlin
Editor: Hennie M. Shore   Photography: David K. Horowitz Studios
Art Director: Charles Brenna   Photography Coordinator: Beth Ann Wakely

INTRODUCTION

Everyone has feelings. Kids, teenagers, grownups—everyone. In the span of just one short hour, our feelings can change many times. We can feel excited about the prospect of a loved one's visit, happy when we think about seeing him or her, stressed about preparing for the visit, disappointed when it is postponed until the coming week, and excited once again about next week's plan.

Children also have many feelings during a given period of time, but they are not always aware of how they are *really* feeling. Often, they are not prepared to deal with their feelings, especially the negative ones. As adults, we are challenged to teach kids about the importance of expressing their feelings so that they will actually feel better about themselves and the world around them.

Children must learn to share how they are feeling with people they trust, and they must learn that by sharing they will better. They must also learn that all feelings—happy, sad, angry, worried, lonely—the list goes on and on—are okay and that expressing them can pave the way toward a healthy lifestyle.

Just as there is a myriad of feelings we experience, we reveal our feelings in many different ways. If we're angry, we shout. If we're happy, we give someone a hug. If we're sad, we cry. But it is our facial expressions that really give us away, and that is the idea behind *Face Your Feelings!*

It's important for kids to recognize how others are feeling by looking at their faces. By understanding the feelings of others, children develop compassion for the people around them. Through this understanding, they become people who are liked and admired by others, people with whom others want to be.

As you read this book with children, or as children read it to themselves, they will learn what actually makes each of the 52 people feel the particular emotion his or her face is expressing. Adults should suggest that children think about all the feelings they have, and then use a mirror to look at their own expressions. It will be useful to them to see how they look when they are angry, or worried, or surprised, so that they can recognize similar expressions in others and react appropriately.

Facing one's feelings can be challenging, but feelings must be dealt with in order to face the ups and downs of life. *Face Your Feelings!* can help.

HAPPY

"I feel happy when
I ride my bike."

HAPPY

"I feel happy when I
have a fun-filled weekend with
my friends."

HAPPY

"I feel happy when
I win a raffle."

HAPPY

"Being with my wife makes me feel happy."

SAD

"I feel sad when a friend is mad at me."

SAD

"I feel sad when people are mean to me and insult me."

SAD

"I feel sad when
I lose a friend."

SAD

"I feel sad when someone I love dies."

LOVING

"I feel loving when I give my mom and dad a hug and kiss good night."

LOVING

"I feel loving when others need love and they need me to love them."

LOVING

"Little children and small animals make me feel loving."

LOVING

"My grandchildren
make me feel loving."

ANGRY

"I feel angry
when someone grabs
something away
from me."

ANGRY

"I feel angry when
someone yells at me
or annoys me."

ANGRY

"Bullies make me angry."

ANGRY

Violence makes
me angry."

SURPRISED

"I feel surprised when someone hollers, 'Surprise!'"

SURPRISED

"I feel surprised when my friends have a surprise party for me."

SURPRISED

"I feel surprised when I get an unexpected call from an old friend."

SURPRISED

"I feel surprised when
an unexpected guest arrives."

SCARED

"Scary movies make
me feel scared."

SCARED

"I feel scared when I'm all alone in a dark, gloomy place."

SCARED

"I feel scared when I have to give a speech to a roomful of people, when I'm taking a test and I haven't studied, when I have more bills than money, and when I read a scary book."

SCARED

"I feel scared when I think about riding on a roller coaster."

CALM

"I feel calm when I'm hugging my blanket and favorite stuffed animal."

CALM

"I feel calm when I'm watching cartoons on Saturday morning."

CALM

"I feel calm when I'm reading
a good book."

CALM

"Sleeping makes
me feel calm."

WORRIED

"I feel worried when
I get in trouble."

WORRIED

"I feel worried when
I'm lost and can't
find my way."

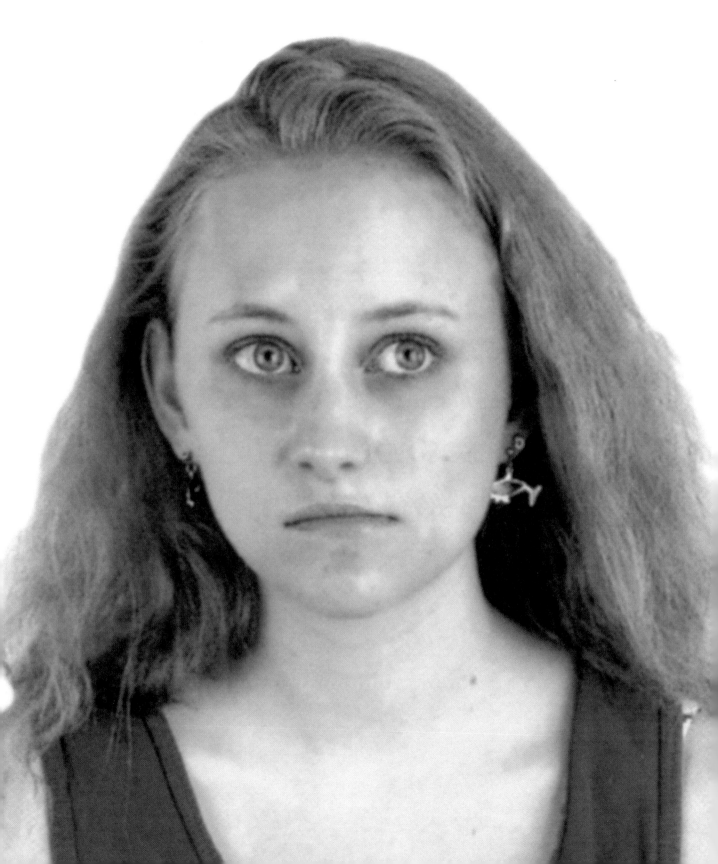

WORRIED

"I feel worried when
I'm unprepared for
something."

WORRIED

"I feel worried when I'm waiting for the results of something important."

EXCITED

"Special events make
me feel excited."

EXCITED

"Parties make me
feel excited."

EXCITED

"I get excited when I think about going on a vacation."

EXCITED

"Fireworks make me
feel excited."

STRESSED

"I feel stressed
when I have to do
something big."

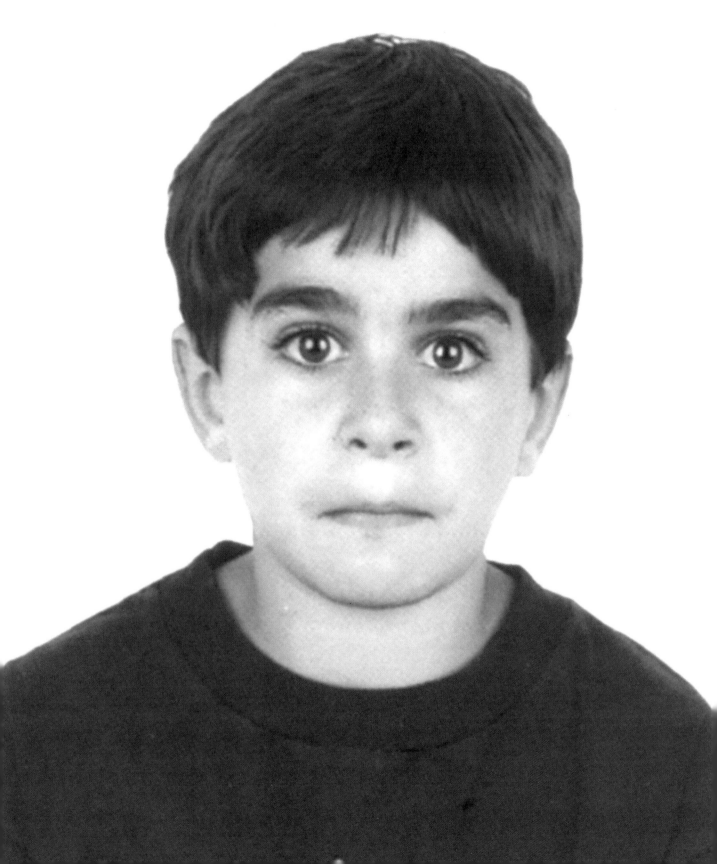

STRESSED

"I feel stressed when I have a lot of schoolwork."

STRESSED

"I feel stressed when something unexpected happens."

STRESSED

"I feel stressed on a day when everything seems to be going wrong."

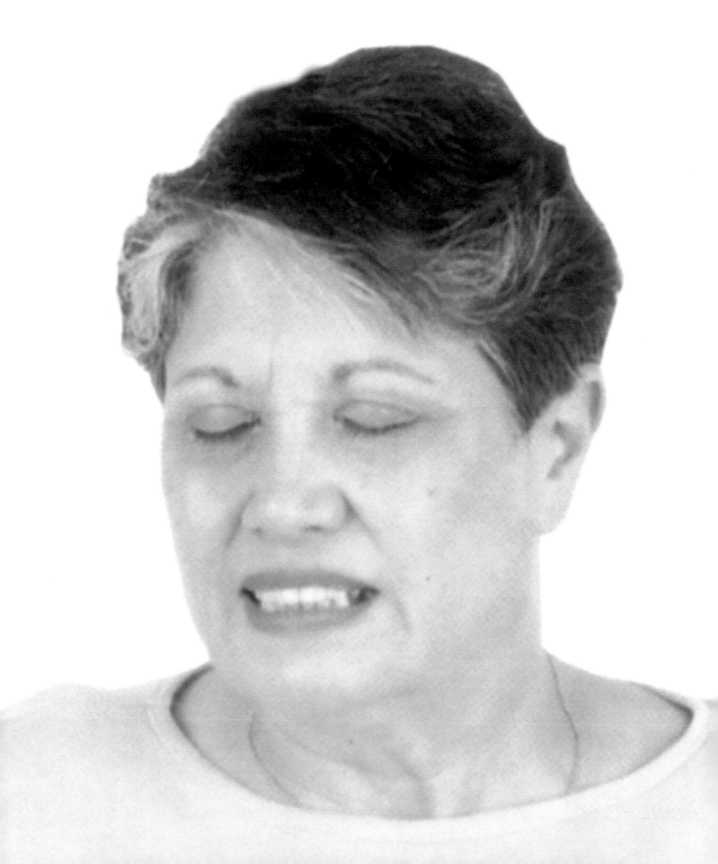

PROUD

"I feel proud when
I get 100% on my spelling
test."

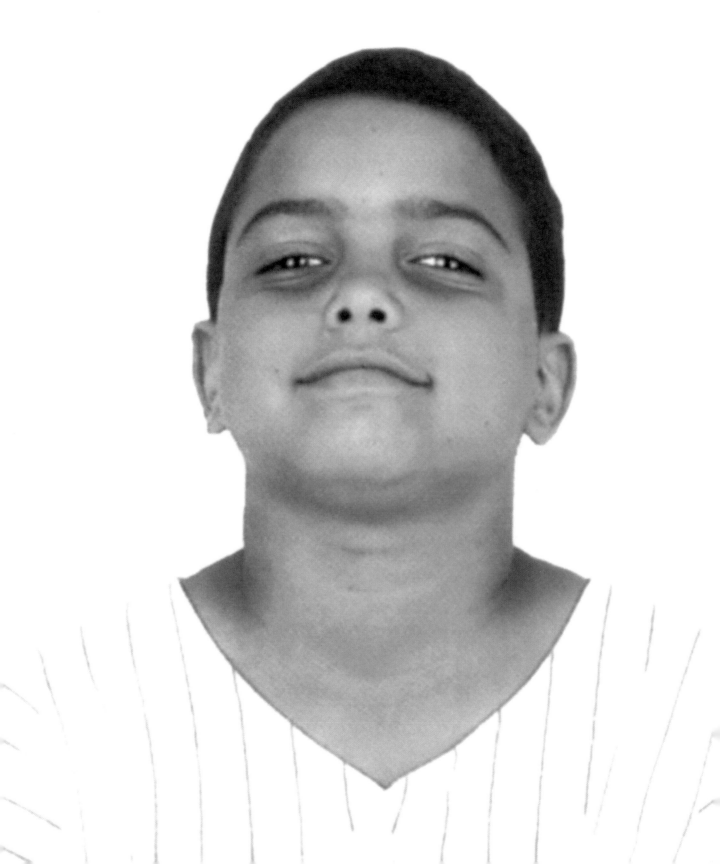

PROUD

"I feel proud when I get a good grade in biology."

PROUD

"I feel proud when I
do a good job."

PROUD

"I feel proud when my children and I achieve."

LONELY

"I feel lonely when I feel like I have no friends."

LONELY

"I feel lonely when I'm
at home studying
by myself."

LONELY

"I feel lonely when something I really wanted to do has been cancelled because there was nobody to do it with."

LONELY

"I feel lonely when my wife's not home."

SILLY

"I feel silly when one
of my friends tells me
a funny joke."

SILLY

"I feel silly when I look
in the mirror."

SILLY

"Being around my friends at work makes me feel silly."

SILLY

"Lots of things make me feel silly–I'll never grow up!"

FACE YOUR FEELINGS!

Think of how you
feel right now and
look in a mirror.

How do *you* look?